Hymns with a Contemporary Touch

Arrangements for Solo Piano
by John Turner

Lillenas PUBLISHING COMPANY
Kansas City, MO 64141

CONTENTS

Be Still, My Soul 4

Have Thine Own Way, Lord 34

He Leadeth Me 10

Lord of the Dance 46

My Jesus, I Love Thee 20

Near the Cross 52

Savior, like a Shepherd Lead Us 30

The Old Rugged Cross 15

There Is a Fountain 42

Were You There? 26

Be Still, My Soul

(Finlandia)

JEAN SIBELIUS
Arranged by John Turner

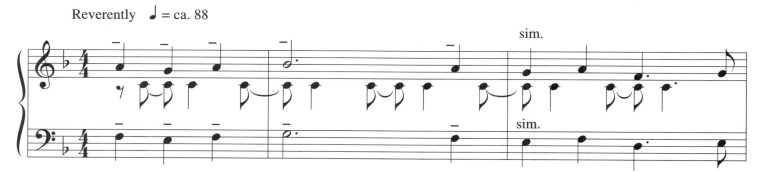

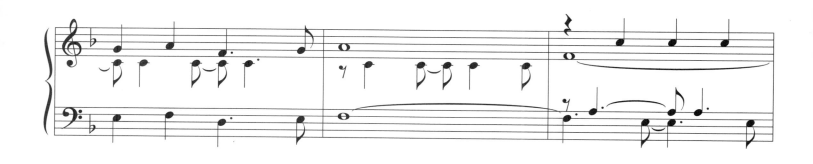

He Leadeth Me

WILLIAM B. BRADBURY
Arranged by John Turner

*Use sustain pedal through first 9 measures to give a distant church bell effect.

melody alternates between r.h. and l.h. until double bar.

The Old Rugged Cross

GEORGE BENNARD
Arranged by John Turner

Gently ♩ = ca. 96

16

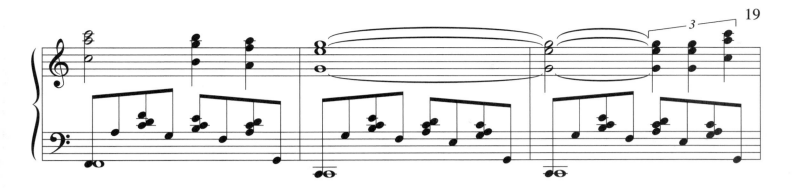

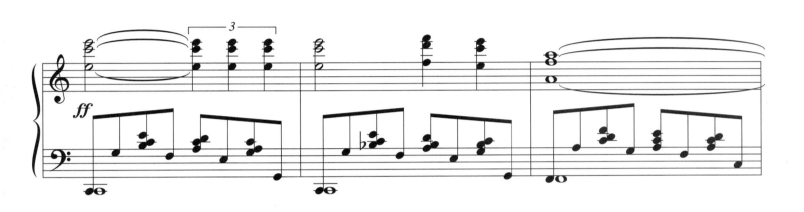

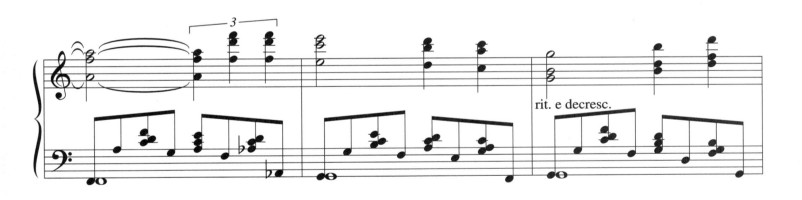

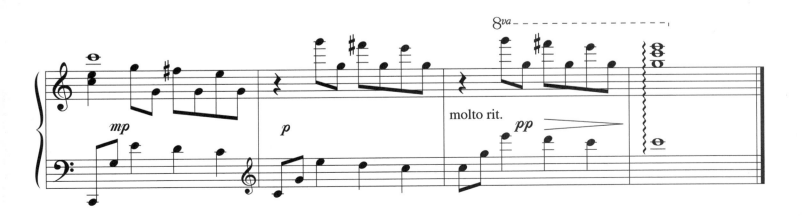

My Jesus, I Love Thee

ADONIRAM J. GORDON
Arranged by John Turner

Were You There?

Afro-American Spiritual
Arranged by John Turner

Rubato, with feeling ♩ = ca. 80

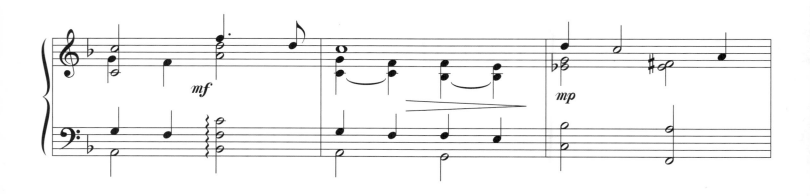

Savior, like a Shepherd Lead Us

WILLIAM B. BRADBURY
Arranged by John Turner

32

Have Thine Own Way, Lord

GEORGE C. STEBBINS
Arranged by John Turner

Lightly   ♩ = ca. 144

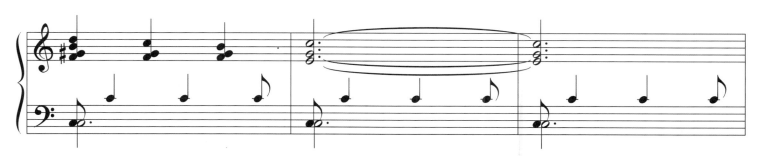

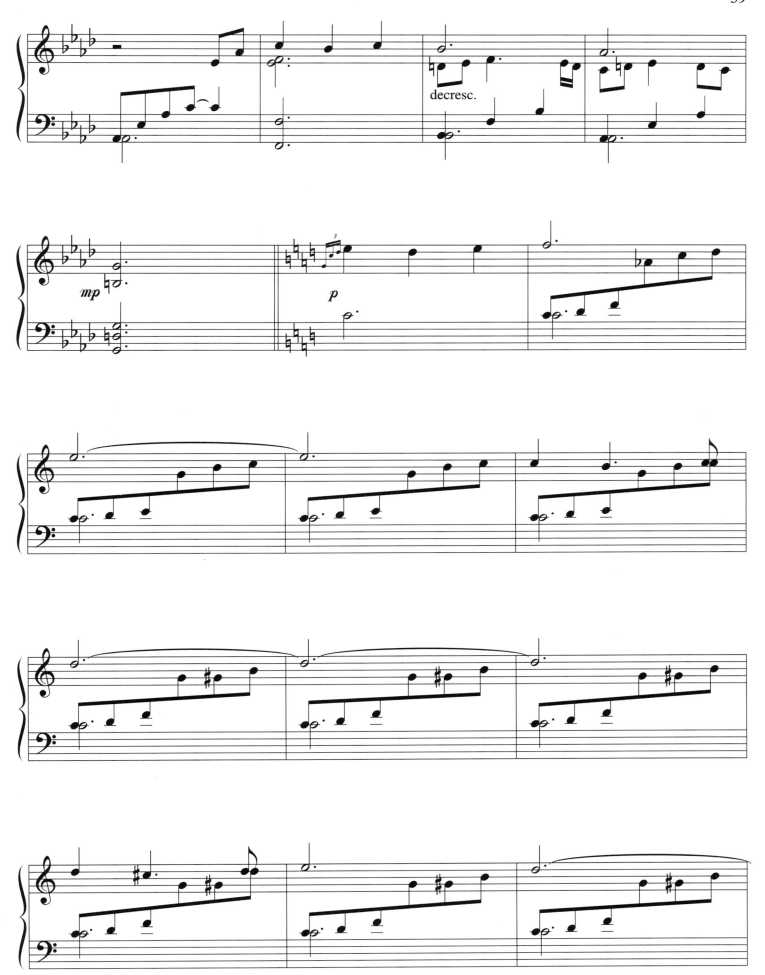

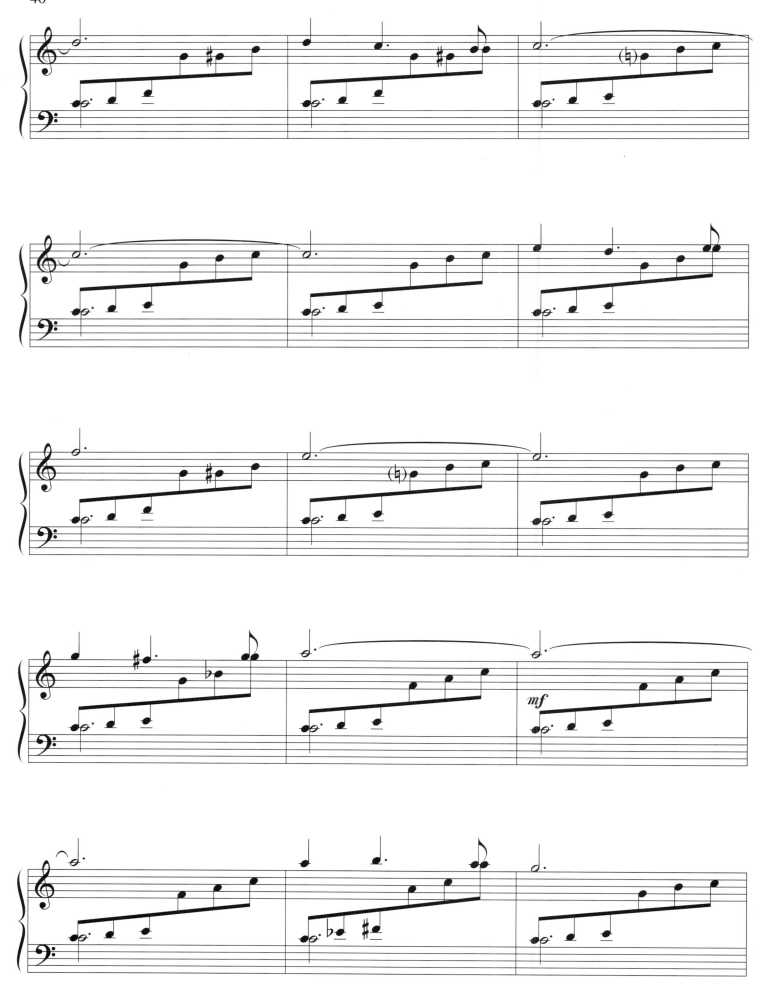

There Is a Fountain

Traditional American Melody
Arranged by John Turner

Lord of the Dance

Shaker Tune
adapted by Sydney Carter
Arranged by John Turner

50

Near the Cross

WILLIAM H. DOANE
Arranged by John Turner

54